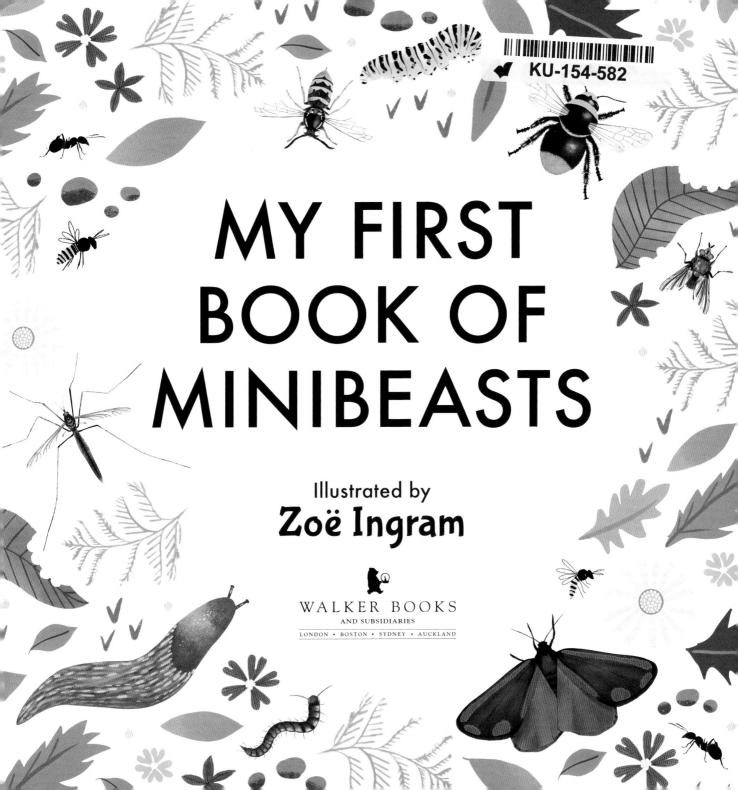

MY FIRST
BOOK OF
MINIBEASTS

Illustrated by
Zoë Ingram

WALKER BOOKS
AND SUBSIDIARIES
LONDON · BOSTON · SYDNEY · AUCKLAND

Minibeast facts

Insect – *Aglais io*	
Lifespan	up to 11 months
Diet	the caterpillars eat nettles; adults drink nectar
Habitat	gardens, meadows and woodland

Did you know?
Unusually for butterflies, adult peacocks can hibernate.

Peacock butterfly

The peacock butterfly is one of the most common garden butterflies. The distinctive "eye" of their markings is to scare off predators, and when their wings are closed they can camouflage with their surroundings. They can produce up to 500 eggs in one go.

Size
63–75 mm

Meadow grasshopper

Grasshopper nymphs hatch in the spring and shed their skins several times before becoming adults in the summer. They rub their legs against their wings to make their famous chirrup call.

Size

17–23 mm

Did you know?
Grasshoppers have their ears on their knees.

Minibeast facts

Insect – *Chorthippus parallelus*

Lifespan	about 1 year
Diet	grass
Habitat	grassland (preferably damp)

Minibeast facts

Insect – *Ephemera danica*

Lifespan	up to 2 years as nymphs; less than 1 day as adults
Diet	nymphs eat aquatic plants and algae; adults don't eat
Habitat	rivers and streams

Did you know?
Female mayflies can lay
up to 8,000 eggs.

Mayfly

Mayflies are among the oldest types of insect on the planet. They spend most of their lives as larvae (or nymphs) underwater, and once they are adults they live for only a few hours – to mate and lay eggs.

Size

15–30 mm

American cockroach

There are over 4,000 different types of cockroach. These unpopular – and smelly – insects are really tough and can survive for a month without food and a week without water. A female cockroach can have over 150 babies in her lifetime.

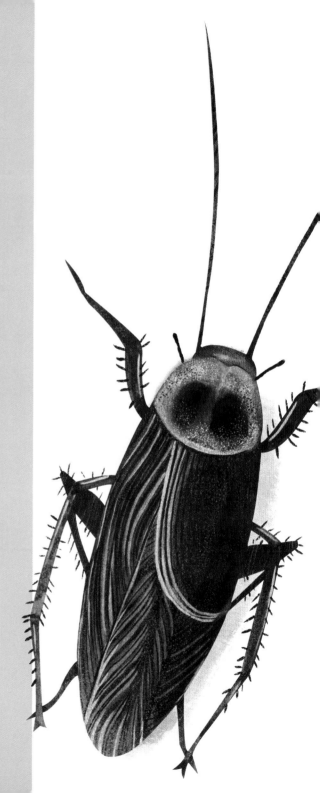

Size
30–50 mm

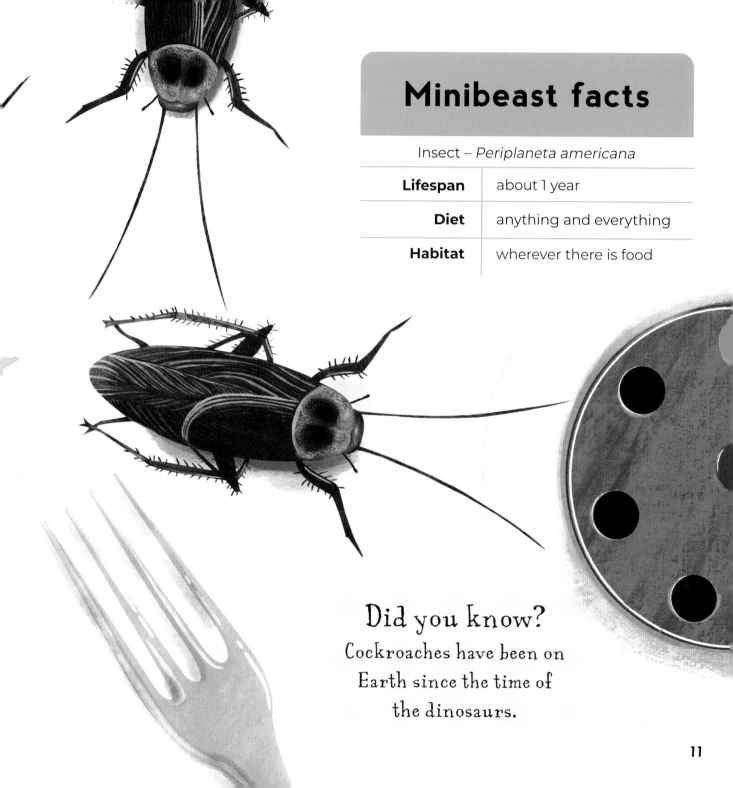

Minibeast facts

Insect – *Periplaneta americana*

Lifespan	about 1 year
Diet	anything and everything
Habitat	wherever there is food

Did you know?
Cockroaches have been on Earth since the time of the dinosaurs.

Minibeast facts

Insect – *Lasius niger*

Lifespan 1–3 years, although queens can live up to 30 years

Diet anything, especially sweet treats

Habitat gardens

Black garden ant

Ants live in large, organized groups called colonies and make their nests in the soil or under stones. They are very strong and have powerful jaws. Ants come from the same family as wasps and bees.

Did you know?
Ants are like dairy farmers – they milk aphids for their honeydew.

Size

5 mm

Crane fly

These large but harmless insects love to flit around in our houses, especially at night-time. Their brown larvae are known as "leatherjackets" and are considered pests because they damage crops.

Size

body 16 mm
legs 50 mm

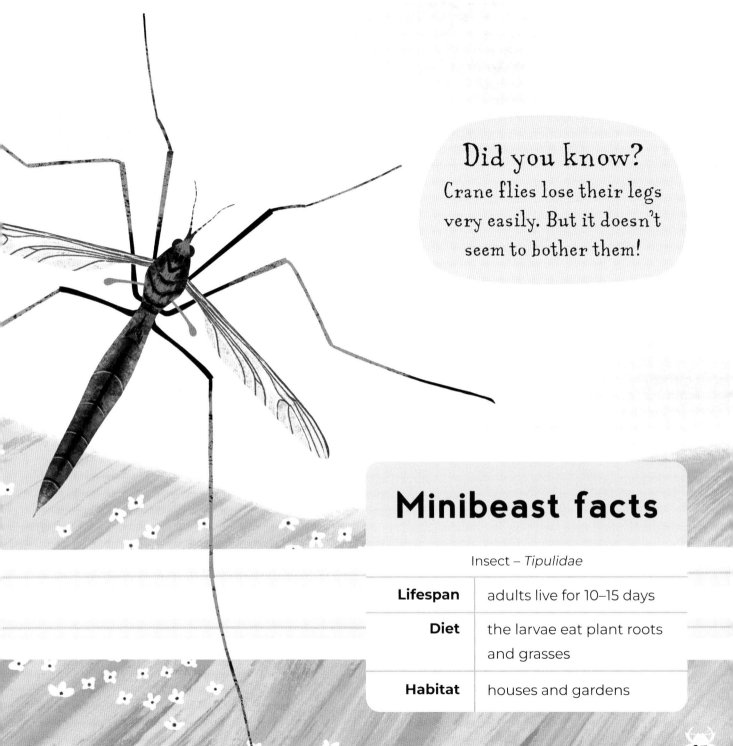

Did you know?
Crane flies lose their legs
very easily. But it doesn't
seem to bother them!

Minibeast facts

Insect – *Tipulidae*

Lifespan	adults live for 10–15 days
Diet	the larvae eat plant roots and grasses
Habitat	houses and gardens

Minibeast facts

Insect – *Tyria jacobaeae*

Lifespan	less than a year
Diet	as caterpillars: leaves and flowers, especially ragwort
Habitat	grassland, woodland and gardens

Did you know?
These moths are named after a red mineral, which used to be used to make the colour vermilion in artists' paint.

Cinnabar moth

This distinctive moth is often mistaken for a butterfly because, unusually, it flies during the day as well as at night. After mating, females lay up to 300 eggs, which hatch as yellow-and-black striped caterpillars. Their bright colours act as a warning to predators.

Size

up to 40 mm

Red-tailed bumblebee

Bumblebees live in large, sociable groups called colonies. They feed on nectar and pollen and are important for spreading pollen between plants, which helps crops grow. Red-tailed bumblebees like to make their nests in the ground.

Size

up to 22 mm

Minibeast facts

Insect – *Bombus lapidarius*	
Lifespan	2–6 weeks; the queen can live up to a year
Diet	nectar and pollen
Habitat	woodland, hedgerows and gardens

Did you know?
An old-fashioned name
for a bumblebee is a
dumbledore.

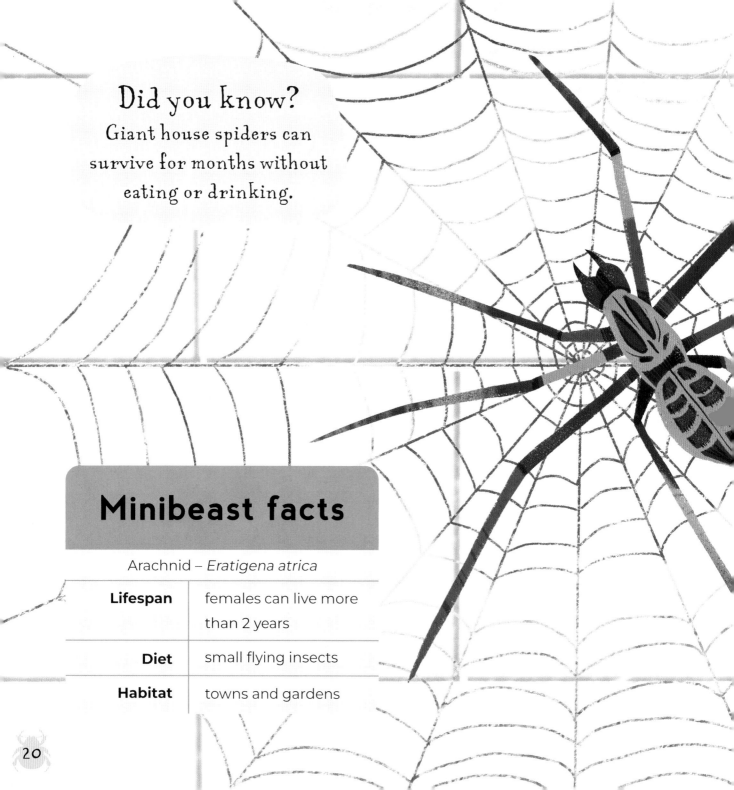

Did you know?
Giant house spiders can survive for months without eating or drinking.

Minibeast facts

Arachnid – *Eratigena atrica*

Lifespan	females can live more than 2 years
Diet	small flying insects
Habitat	towns and gardens

Giant house spider

Most often seen in autumn, these spiders have eight very long legs and can run very fast. They build thick webs in the corners of rooms to trap their prey and have tiny hairs on their legs that help them sense their surroundings.

Size
legspan 25–75 mm

Glow-worm

Glow-worms are not worms at all – they're beetles. Only the female actually glows: her tail lights up in the dark (with bioluminescence) to help her attract a mate. She lays up to 100 eggs, which take about two years to become adults.

Size

25 mm

Did you know?
The glow of a glow-worm can be seen from up to 50 metres away.

Minibeast facts

Insect – *Lampyris noctiluca*

Lifespan	up to 2 years as larvae; a few weeks as adults
Diet	the larvae eat slugs and snails
Habitat	grassland, hedgerows and woodland

Minibeast facts

Gastropod – *Arion hortensis*

Lifespan	up to 6 years
Diet	plants, leaves and earthworms
Habitat	gardens

Did you know?
Slug blood is green.

Garden slug

Most people think of slugs as pests, but they are important recyclers of decaying plants. By eating rotting vegetation, they help keep the soil healthy for growing crops. Slugs breathe through a hole just behind their heads. They like cool, damp places and mostly come out at night. Slugs' slime is actually a liquid crystal.

Size

up to 30 mm

Centipede

Brown centipedes have fifteen pairs of legs, one pair for each body segment. They spend most of the day hiding under stones and dead wood and come out at night to hunt for prey, which they kill with their venomous front legs.

Size

30 mm

Minibeast facts

Chilopod – *Lithobius forficatus*	
Lifespan	5–6 years
Diet	other invertebrates
Habitat	woodland, grassland and gardens

Did you know?
Centipedes can walk backwards as quickly as they can walk forwards.

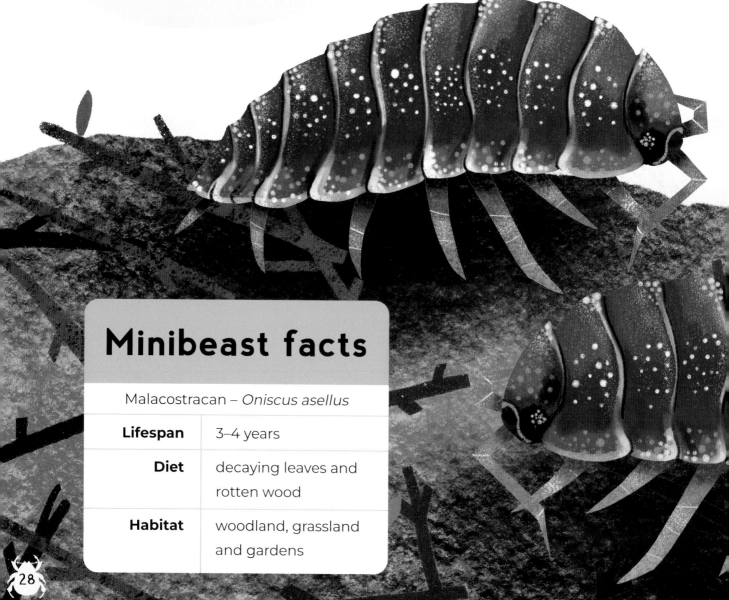

Did you know?
Woodlice breathe through
gills – just like fish!

Minibeast facts

Malacostracan – *Oniscus asellus*

Lifespan	3–4 years
Diet	decaying leaves and rotten wood
Habitat	woodland, grassland and gardens

Woodlouse

The woodlouse is a crustacean, which means it is related to the crab family. Its body is made up of lots of segments and it has seven pairs of legs. When it is frightened, it curls into a tight ball and is protected by its armoured shell.

Size

up to 18 mm

Bluebottle

This large, common fly gets its name from its shiny, blue body. Bluebottles have a very loud buzz and are often found near the bodies of dead animals, where they lay their eggs. Once hatched, the maggots feed from this site for days.

Size

10–14 mm

Minibeast facts

Insect – *Calliphora vomitoria*

Lifespan   about 6 weeks

Diet   the maggots eat decaying plants and carrion

Habitat   near rivers in warmer months and in towns in the winter

Did you know?
Bluebottles eat their food twice.

Minibeast facts

Insect – *Papilio machaon*

Lifespan	3–4 weeks as a caterpillar
Diet	milk parsley
Habitat	fenland

Did you know?
Young swallowtail caterpillars look just like bird droppings.

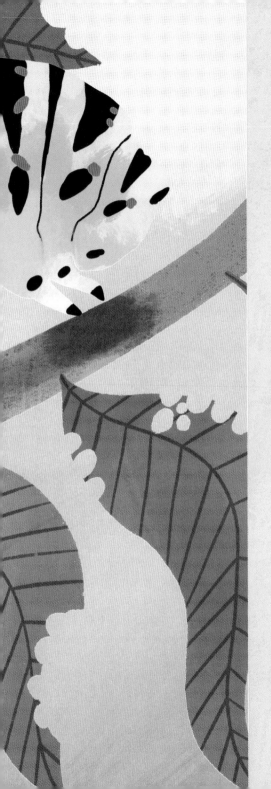

Swallowtail caterpillar

A caterpillar is the larva of a butterfly or a moth. It hatches from an egg and spends most of its life eating and growing. It sheds its skin four or five times as it grows. After a few weeks, it turns into a pupa (or chrysalis) before finally emerging as a butterfly.

Size

up to 50 mm

Snail

Garden snails carry their homes on their backs and love a shady spot. Their bodies are made of one big muscle, called a "foot". They lay about 80 eggs at a time. The newly hatched snails take two years to fully grow up. Snail shells nearly always curl clockwise.

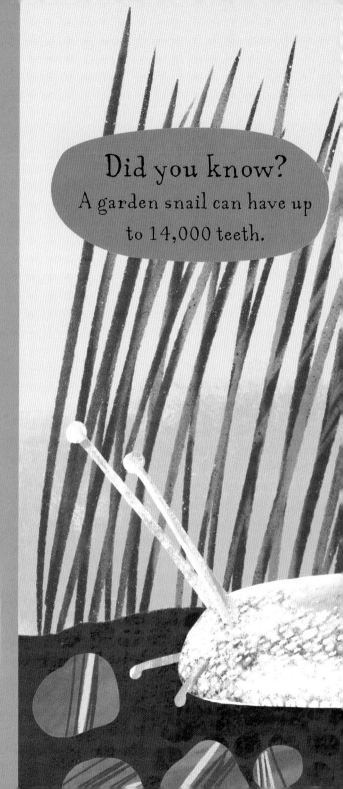

Did you know?
A garden snail can have up to 14,000 teeth.

Size

shell up to 40 mm

Minibeast facts

Gastropod – *Helix aspersa*	
Lifespan	2–3 years
Diet	leaves and rotting vegetation
Habitat	woodland, grassland and gardens

Minibeast facts

Insect – *Carabus violaceus*	
Lifespan	as larvae for 10 months; as adults for 9 months
Diet	slugs, worms and insects
Habitat	woodland, hedgerows and gardens

Did you know?
Ground beetles can't
fly, but they can run
very quickly.

Violet ground beetle

The violet ground beetle is a large, shiny beetle that lives under logs and stones and mostly comes out at night. Adult females lay up to 600 eggs at a time in soil, and the larvae live underground until they are ready to emerge as beetles.

Size

30 mm

Emperor dragonfly

Emperor dragonflies are one of the largest species of dragonfly. The males have blue bodies and the females are green. They have two pairs of wings and catch their food while flying in the air. Young dragonflies are called nymphs.

Size

wingspan 120 mm

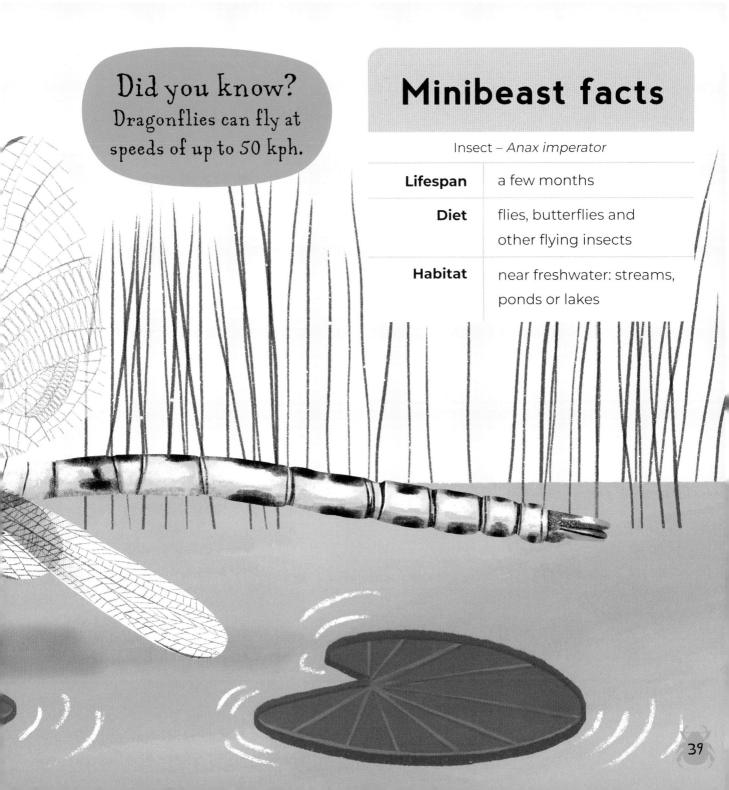

Did you know?
Dragonflies can fly at
speeds of up to 50 kph.

Minibeast facts

Insect – *Anax imperator*

Lifespan	a few months
Diet	flies, butterflies and other flying insects
Habitat	near freshwater: streams, ponds or lakes

Minibeast facts

Clitellate – *Lumbricus terrestris*	
Lifespan	4–8 years
Diet	decaying plant and animal matter, funghi, soil
Habitat	anywhere there is soil

Did you know?
Earthworms have five hearts.

Earthworm

Earthworms eat a third of their weight in dead leaves every day, which helps to keep soil healthy for us to grow food in. They come to the surface when it rains and are a valuable source of food for birds and wild animals.

Size

100–250 mm

41

Wasp

Although wasps are unpopular, they are extremely useful for pollination and for keeping other pests under control. They live in large groups, in nests made out of wood that has been chewed up by the queen. They build these in houses and roofs. They sting to protect themselves from danger.

Size

workers: **11–14 mm**
queens: **20–25 mm**

Minibeast facts

Insect – *Vespula vulgaris*

Lifespan	workers 12–22 days; queens up to a year
Diet	nectar, fruit and picnics; the young are fed insects and spiders
Habitat	gardens, woodland and grassland

Did you know?
Wasps live everywhere except Antarctica.

Index

Tick off the creatures that you have seen in your home, garden or out and about.

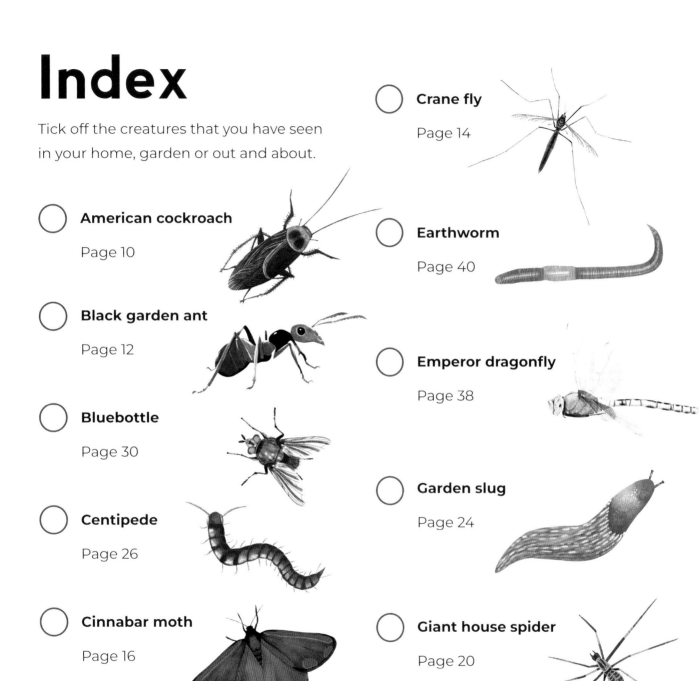

**This book is dedicated to my
millipede-loving biggest kiddo.
And Janey and Nina.**

First published 2022 by Walker Books Ltd
87 Vauxhall Walk, London SE11 5HJ
This edition published 2023 for Scottish Book Trust
Scottish charity, SC07668

2 4 6 8 10 9 7 5 3 1

This book has been typeset in Futura,
Montserrat, Nevis and Aunt Mildred

Printed in China

British Library Cataloguing in Publication Data:
a catalogue record for this book is available
from the British Library

ISBN 978-1-5295-1920-4

www.walker.co.uk

Also by Zoë Ingram:

MY FIRST BOOK OF BIRDS

Illustrated by Zoë Ingram

978-1-4063-9418-4

MY FIRST BOOK OF WOODLAND ANIMALS

Illustrated by Zoë Ingram

978-1-4063-9157-2

MY FIRST BOOK OF SEA CREATURES

Illustrated by Zoë Ingram

978-1-5295-0408-8

MY FIRST BOOK OF DINOSAURS

WITH 20 DINOSAURS

Illustrated by Zoë Ingram

978-1-5295-0997-7

Available from all good booksellers

www.walker.co.uk